IN[...]

CW00540943

TREES DON'T GO TO SCHOOL

rees don't go to school,
Won't sit still and shut up
And muck about lots.
Trees are messy,
Don't grow in straight lines and neat rows,
Never comb their hair
And once a year
They dare to cover our clean concrete streets
With their dirty brown leaves!
Trees definitely deserve detentions!

Trees tell terrible jokes,
But you're not a tree.
So you wouldn't understand.
So I won't tell you.
So there!

Trees keep on growing,
NO matter how much you shout at them
Or punish them,
But in the end,
Just like you
They can be hurt.

**"Daydreaming again little Larch?
When the head hears of this
He'll chop you into little bits!
I won't be surprised when he cuts you down to size.
Out with the chainsaw
And little Larchy is no more!
In ten days time you'll be shiny and neat,
Finishing your life as a wooden toilet seat!"**

1

A

Hang on a second...
Trees have had enough!
We will not be sat on anymore!
Trees on truant!
NO MORE **SCHOOL** !!
We want to wake with the soft dawn,
Let the sun melt us into day,
Hear the birds sing inside us.

NO MORE **SCHOOL** !!
We want to huddle and
Cuddle in the rain,

Write poems a hundred feet high,
Stay awake way after bedtime,
And
    Fall
      Into
        Faery-land

Trees on truant!
If you keep cutting us down,
We'll hold our breath
Until the world turns blue
And no-one can breathe.

WE INTERRUPT THIS POEM TO BRING YOU AN EMERGENCY NEWSFLASH!

      ''Yesterday it was reported that a young beech tree was caught streaking stark naked through the quiet streets of Winter. One blind resident complained, '**Ugh! All those rude branches dancing nude in the wind, with not even a leaf to cover herself! It's disgusting and shouldn't be allowed!**' Miss Tree said in her defense, '**It's totally natural! All this fuss is a mystery to me!**' The government has reacted by issuing a standard set of white cotton underpants to every tree in the country. Families may now take their children to forests, but it is advised to wear dark glasses. More details later...''

DARK

2

EGG POEM

I am an egg,
With only one leg,
On which for my living I beg.

I tell terrible jokes
All about yolks,
And when folks don't laugh,
I hoppit!

3

AND

WHEN
THE
HOUSE
FELT
LONELY,
HE
SHUT
ALL
THE
DOORS
AND
STAYED
AT
HOME
THAT
NIGHT

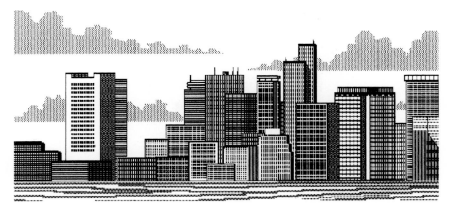

GLOOMY

A gorilla sits
And stares at the wall.

Big,
Black,
A brain that is enormous;
Pools of eyes
Drowning in sadness.

The gorilla in the zoo
Is looking at you.
Will you tap the glass?
Try to make him laugh?

Ten foot
By
Ten foot
Of sculptured concrete
For his huge feet.

He dreams of leaves
Bigger than a newspaper
And walking through greenness
For a hundred miles in a straight line
Without stopping.

Now
He
Walks
A
Hundred
Miles
Ten
Foot
At
A
Time

PARAGRAPH

DAUGHTER

Hot sun soak her up.
Cold cloud feeling grey, fed up
Spit her out
With a shout of thunder how she falls!
falls asleep
lies deep.

Mountains weep and dream
and in the dream she dances,
seems to grow
stronger, longer
full of river longing, wide awake,
thrills like a milkshake shivers,
She spills into the land.

But then a man-made hand
stops her dead with a dam.
Down
     Down
          Down underground
pushed around by tubes of steel
in this rushing endless maze,
amazing nightmare drowning deep
whirled around by endless fists of metal
how she weeps.

Someone twists the tap
tap, kettle, cup of tea
into me and
out of me
down the drain
underground
rushing round
full of longing
wide awake
she spills into the land
filling out the sea
where the hot sun waits

How she sings!

SAINSBURY'S LOVE POEM

I'm in love with Sainsbury's Brand Sausages
I'm in love with Sainsbury's Brand Spam.

Will you be my one kilogramme of washed sultanas,
Unbleachèd?
Will you be my catering margerine with E331
For some additive fun?

Ah! My little pack of processed cheese,
I hear a harmony when frozen chickens sing to you
warble, warble, warble
cluck, cluck cluck.

At night,
Refrigeration units hum
sing lullaby,
sing lullaby.
Then,
The whole store comes alive,
That flavoured joghurt-jelly-gelatine-jive!

Oh! My little can of creamy milk,
Condensed,
I love thee so!

WE

SNICKERY SNICKERY DOO

Snickery Snickery Doo
i love Jane,
i really do.
yesterday, I pecked her on the cheek,
she slapped me with her lovely hand,
she said to me,
wot a cheek!
now don't you be so randy,
my Pandy Andy!

Snickery Snickery Doo
now i'm in love with you.

i fancy her.
in fact,
i fancy that she fancies me!
fancy that?
you fancy that?
you better not, or you'll be in trouble,
'cos Jane is my sweetest, neatest bubble of champagne!
in fact she's well allright by me,
allright?

Snickery Snickery Doo
love, love, love,
do be do be do.

THE DREAM OF THE ROOF

I have sat for many
Risings of the sun and
Fallings of the moon
And have been a good cap
On the head of this house.
I keep him warm when
Winter sings around me.
Men built me well
For never have I been scared
Of the wild wind,
Even in her greatest anger,
When she tears the clouds like paper.
Nothing is colder than the
Shower that falls on me,
When the sky weeps.

Still I stand,
Until the sun comes again
And I am shining like a great jewel in my wet coat.

Then, the city is a place where magic lives.
And we are washed clean of all dirt....
Until Time itself grew up
And men grew into children,
Withered and old children with closed hearts.

I heard their voices,
I who lay myself over people's heads.
As they opened their mouths,
To fill them full of shouting,
It was not the song of the wind
But a cold sound.

FOLLOWED

Fighting, I do not understand.
Every tile, every beam, every cross-nail of me
Has joined together to make me what I am.
If nail said to beam,
I don't want to be here!
Surely, I should laugh at his childishness.
Together, we keep out the cold,
Apart and broken,
We are nothing.

When the fighting started,
My drain-pipes filled with tears to overflowing.
When the bombs began to drop
Like metal clouds from the sky,
I felt fear for the first time.

I wanted to shout,
But had no mouth.
I wished to run,
But had no legs.
Men built me.
Now,
Men would destroy me.....

One bomb fell,
And then I dreamed of flying,
exploding like a great shoal of white gulls
Into the air,
And then I dreamed no more.

THE

10

STREET SIGNS

DEAD SLOW CHILDREN!
And there they were!
Forty-three children crawling down the middle of the road
On their hands and knees!
Dead slow and dead boring!

I turned left.
Big mistake!
Straight ahead,
A sign said,
MEN AT WORK!
Never seen anything stranger -
Thousands of frowning men
Spilling into the road
In grey suits, grey ties and grey shoes -
Sitting at grey desks and scribbling furiously!
The whole high street was blocked,
I had to swerve to miss them....

At last, a smooth road!
Reassuring traffic lights -
Red, Yellow, Green,
FORK AHEAD!
I must be going mad!
A fifty foot fork pronging the sky
With a sausage the size of a house on the end!
I couldn't take it anymore and had to park on the Side.
Sayid said to me,
"Do you mind!?"
Yes I did mind,
But by that time, I'd lost my mind.
It was the last straw.

DIVERSION AHEAD!
And right by the sign,
A Juggler,
A Clown,
And a Fool who came up to me
To whisper in my troubled ear,
"Don't believe everything you read!!!"

11

SNORING

My brother's snoring
Makes such a sound!
It shakes the bed
And shivers the ground.
I never get any sleep,
Not even a peep
Because of that creep....

So I stick my two big toes
Right up his nose!
It's the best way to stop him, I've found!

WITHOUT

POEM FOR THE VERBALLY CONFUSED

Got up,
BOILED the bed,
Took the train down the stairs,
Feeling live-tired and with such a baking head!
Drank not one shredded wheat, but three.
Then I Grew myself a nice cup of tea,

PLANTED some toast, Watered the eggs,
Sat down in a chair and Ate my legs!
Had to Crush my teeth and Smash my face,
Poached my hair until it looked dead ace!

After I **DUG** my way to boring school,
Went for a snog in the local Snogging Pool.

CAUGHT the bus, Put it in my pocket,
My mum Made a fuss and Told me to Return it.

Then I had to **KILL** my homework, which was very satisfying,
Especially when all the answers were Writhing round and
Dying!

In the end,
I Pounded into bed,
CUT off my weary head
And Swam down deep
Into soft and silent sleep.....

PLEASE
TAKE
GENEROUSLY

13

FQR EVER AND EVER

Said the Mountain,
I shall live for ever.
Then came wind,
Came rain woven in weather,
And the mountain crumbled.

Said the Wind,
I am here! There!
Dancing always in a dress of Air!
Then Earth turned still
And wind was humbled.

Said the Sea,
When mountains weep,
I fall down deep,
Until Sun drank,
And into Her mouth sea tumbled.

Said the Fire,
I shall climb the sky
And live up high!
So the flames sang
As clouds rumbled.

Said the Man,
I can carve mountains
As if they were ice,
Ride the air
Like a winged horse,
Walk on water,
Only wood beneath me,
Set fire to my enemy and smile....

And Man was not humbled
Until his empty heart rumbled,
The cities tumbled
And the Earth it crumbled
Away.

WHAT I SAID ONE DAY

Pass the salt, please!

No.

Could I have some more?

No.

Any Chance of a cup of tea?

No.

Could I please use your toilet?

No.

Do you want to come out and play?

No.

Is that all you can say?

Yes.

Will you be my friend?

No.

Allright then....

Missile
Missile
Guess I'll miss you when you're gone

Weapon
Weapon
Weep on the land

Missile
Missile
Missiles raining down
Had to get out of the storm
Hell of a show
Got completely legless

A just war
Just a war
'Go on Dad! Just a little war!
Please! It is for peace, honest!
Cross my heart and hope to die!'
Oh, allright then son!

HE

things

Tom had the best collection in the class,
Of marbles, Blue Stars and Frosted Spiders of glass.
Sold them to the infants for a mountain of money.

Next, He turned to Phil-At-Ely,
His stamps such quiet friends, always there.
They couldn't turn their backs,
But only smiled with a colour so rare.

He jumped on the skateboard just for a dare,
It helped him make a smooth get-away,
Slipped through the silent, polyurethane night
Out of the hurt of the bright, bright day.

His mum, who tried so hard, would always say
When he cried, *Here's some money, buy something nice.*
So, he locked his tears in a box of ice,

And went to the shops once or twice,
But he only learned to spend
And never found a friend.

Tom grew into a grown-up in the end,
Computers, a house, marriage, fame.
Now he had learned to play the game.

And there is no-one he can ever blame
For the hurt inside,
he tried so hard, for so long to hide.

<u>yesterday, I fell in love with myself</u>

Yesterday, I fell in love with myself.
We started going everywhere together.
People noticed of course,
And many of them were jealous.
But they all agreed it was a good thing
And made sound economic sense -
Similar incomes, ideas, goals.

They said we ought to go into politics,
Such love could serve the world!
So we did, Me and I,
Held hands to hold the world in our caring grip.

Then, what we feared came true.
It appeared that other people appeared
To be falling in love with themselves.
At first, it didn't seem to matter.
Business in the city was still brisk,
Only the Pound was quiet overnight.

Yet the mutterings had begun.
In park squares,
On wooden benches,
They were all talking to themselves.
It was very embarrassing,
Especially the noise of their love-making.

For, by now our love was neat,
Silent, economical, discreet.
Bans were enforced with justifiable violence,
Which made sound political sense.

Me and I were married in the end,
My best man, my Self, my only friend.
Together Triumphant Trinity,
How we ran this Great and Glorious Country
Down.

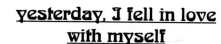

SOMETIMES IT'S ALL SO AMAZING

Sometimes it's all so amazing,
I want to fall at the feet of every singing pigeon,
Shopkeepers' conversation seems positively Shakespearean
And the sweet wrappers that flower down the street
Are perfectly arranged.

Sometimes it's all so amazing,
I could watch a tree like a TV,
Every leaf a brilliant documentary,
Each shadow as riveting as Inspector Morse.

Sometimes it's all so amazing,
I'll say kind things to people I can't even stand,
Look for the good in their face, heart and hand,
And find it.

Sometimes it's all so amazing,
Every day becomes a holy-day.
I could even pray
To bacon and eggs,
And a cup of tea is a spiritual experience!

Sometimes it's all so amazing,
I could say hello to a complete stranger,
Look into his eyes, let go my forever fear of danger
And just for a second, he would become my deepest friend.

when i grow up, i want to be as tall as a

MOUNTAIN

but what if I should fall

O
F
F
?

A THROW AWAY POEM

I'm the Rubbish-Man,
Prince of Plastic, King of Tin Can.
People say I'm disgusting,
But the children are so trusting
When I rip {*or do they throw?*}
Such sweet wrappers out of their hands
To scatter them brightly across the lands.

I am the Reveller of Rags,
Emperor of Empty Shopping Bags.

Yes! I'm the Rubbish Man!
Catch me, Collar me, Collect me if you can.
It's me who stole into your sleep,
Took your mattress soft and deep.
Now, I'm coiled up, comfortably rusting by the Rubbish Stream
As She slips her way through the city's dark dream.

Oh! I'm the Rubbish Man!
Rubbing out wishes as only I can.
I made the blocks that burn the sky
And if you dare to ask me why,
I'll say it's my job, it's what I do.
Then will I dance The Rubbish Dance for you.

For, I'm the Rubbish Man!
Bin me, Bag me, Beat me if you can,
But together we'll dance all days away
And Darkness, my friend, shall come to stay.

37

HAD

GONE

work hard

He could go far, if only he would work hard.

I had been reported.
Next term, I tried to work hard,
Hard as a black road
Cut between the cars and the grass,
Hard as the nail that stole suddenly into wood,
Hard as Superman, the man of steel
Who lived on paper;
As hard as the best of the best,
The beans of the beans;
Harder than A and B
Hard as a C or even D
And sometimes the hardest, an E.

My alphabet was never good enough.
I worked hard as a house of cards,
But then it toppled,
Tumbling tears and I cried...

Cry Baby! Cry Baby! Na-na-na-na-na!
Softy! Softy! Softy-Softy-Softy!
What a woman! What a woman!

Being soft as a woman didn't work either.
So, instead of working hard,
I became hard;
Hard as boots, skinny trousers, skinny hair;
Hard as a stare.
And I ran from A,B, C, D and E
To live my life beginning with F,
If you know what I mean.

At last, I was the man of steel,
With a stolen boy inside.
That was hard, and lonely.
My skin was so tough though,
At last, like a snake I slipped out,
To grow into this man
With a woman in his heart.

LEAVING

I AM IN LOVE WITH ANN ELBOW

I met a Foot the other day.
We shook Toes.
I met a Nose not so long ago
And blew her a sloppy kiss.
Ever seen a Nose blush?
A Nostril flush?

Last night,
I met a pair of Eyes,
Hanging out behind the lids.
Shifty twins,
And right by their side
A nosy pair of Ears!
I really had to Leggit!

I met a Mouth this morning.
By Gum, he gave me lip!
And that cheeky Bum was so rude!
The Ankle Sisters such a strain
And when I met the Head,
She was a pain in the neck!

Just now,
I asked Anne Atter-Active Leg for a date,
But she stood me up
And now I'm so confused!

LAST NIGHT I SAW THE CITY BREATHING

LAST night, I saw the City breathing:
Great Gusts of people,
Rushing in and
Puffing out
Of Stations' singing mouths

Last night, I saw the City laughing.
Take-Aways got the giggles,
Cinemas split their sides,
And Living Rooms completely creased themselves!

Last night, I saw the City dance.
Shadows were cheek to cheek with brick walls,
Trains wiggled their hips all over the place,
And the trees
In the breeze,
Put on a show for an audience of windows!

Last night, I saw the city starving,
Snaking Avenue smacked her lips
And swallowed seven roundabouts!
Fat office blocks got stuffed with light
And gloated over empty parking lots.

ONLY

LAST night, I saw the City crying.
Cracked windows poured falling stars
And the streets were paved with mirrors.

Last night, I saw the City sit down at last.
Armchairs cuddled up to warm human beings
And a million cups of tea
Made best freinds with a million pairs of hands.

Last night, I saw the City sleeping
Roads night-dreamed,
Street Lamps quietly boasted,
'When I grow up, I'm going to be a star!'
And the Wind,
Like a cat,
Snoozed in the nooks of roofs.

AN

FOR MARC
{with love}

For when my brother dies
I shall cry tears of stone
Never will I have felt so alone
And my heart will try to be hard

For when my brother dies,
No more late night Monopoly and after
Bacon and eggs with a cup of laughter
The yolk of dawn just breaking

For when my brother dies
I shall cry a city of tears
Then put on a smile, hide all my fears
If only I could, if only

For when my brother dies
No more hate and family spite
Now I'm fine, everything's all right
But I will miss the making up

For when my brother dies
I shall cry blades of grass
People will be polite, dare not ask
Why my garden overgrows

For when my brother dies
I shall have no brother
No other to hug and to hold
And I the younger,
shall be the one who will grow old

POEMUM

NO MUM!

DON'T!

NO, NO NOT THE CHECKOUT ASSISTANT

PLeeeeeeeeeeeeeeeeeeeeeeeeeeASE!

I GO TINNED TOMATO RED

WHEN SHE TALKS TO ANYONE

We're walking down the street and
AAAAAAAAAAAAAAAAAAAARGH!!!!
SHE'S SAYING SOMETHING FUNNY TO

A WOMAN WITH A DOG

IT'S REALLY LOUD

I HOPE NOBODY TURNS ROUND.....

I GO GREEN AS A LETTUCE

MARK!

I WISH I WAS AS SMALL AS A LETTUCE

EVERYDAY SAYINGS

I married a door, how he screeched and whinged
Just couldn't handle it, became unhinged.

Married a chair, unlike any fable
He kept ending up under the table.

Married a mirror, you know, just to see!
He wasn't all he was cracked up to be.

So I fell in love with a tall, dark Cliff!
It was a long

Only I had stuck with Paperback Man,
Spineless! All words, ended like it began.

So, I hung out with a cute Coat-Hanger;
He was hung up, no more shall I hanker.

At last! I met the Curtain of my dreams.
It seems I was attracted to his seams.

Love drew us together, A love cloth-soft
Love could not be contained nor curtained off.
Love folded as night with rings for binding
Enfold us tonight, morning for finding
You...

THIS

BALLAD OF THE TREES

In your words, I am an Oak tree,
And I have been here a hundred years
Or more.
They tried to put me away in an old people's
home,
But I'm still hanging about in the street like a
tramp,
The earth is a good bed and
My blanket the wide sky.

Once,
I was round, small as your thumb
Until my mother dropped me,
Just like that.
I fell to the ground,
A dream inside a seed,
Waiting.

Then,
This street was stripped of its bark
And underneath lay the muddy drover's path.
Horses ploughed your classroom and
Barley grew between your desks.
It is so easy to forget.

Now,
In your words,
I am grown old.
The concrete hides me away,
And the street tries to run me over.
I wrap myself in bark
Against this biting wind.

But if you stop
And listen,
I shall promise to sing you a song of leaves
And if you dream,
Dream the cold hearted cities away, away
Dream the cold hearted cities away.

Missile
Missile
Guess I'll miss you when you're gone

Weapon
Weapon
Weep on the land

Missile
Missile
Missiles raining down
Had to get out of the storm
Hell of a show
Got completely legless

A just war
Just a war
'Go on Dad! Just a little war!
Please! It is for peace, honest!
Cross my heart and hope to die!'
Oh, allright then son!

HE

things

Tom had the best collection in the class,
Of marbles, Blue Stars and Frosted Spiders of glass.
Sold them to the infants for a mountain of money.

Next, He turned to Phil-At-Ely,
His stamps such quiet friends, always there.
They couldn't turn their backs,
But only smiled with a colour so rare.

He jumped on the skateboard just for a dare,
It helped him make a smooth get-away,
Slipped through the silent, polyurethane night
Out of the hurt of the bright, bright day.

His mum, who tried so hard, would always say
When he cried, *Here's some money, buy something nice.*
So, he locked his tears in a box of ice,

And went to the shops once or twice,
But he only learned to spend
And never found a friend.

Tom grew into a grown-up in the end,
Computers, a house, marriage, fame.
Now he had learned to play the game.

And there is no-one he can ever blame
For the hurt inside,
he tried so hard, for so long to hide.

<u>yesterday, I fell in love with myself</u>

Yesterday, I fell in love with myself.
We started going everywhere together.
People noticed of course,
And many of them were jealous.
But they all agreed it was a good thing
And made sound economic sense -
Similar incomes, ideas, goals.

They said we ought to go into politics,
Such love could serve the world!
So we did, Me and I,
Held hands to hold the world in our caring grip.

Then, what we feared came true.
It appeared that other people appeared
To be falling in love with themselves.
At first, it didn't seem to matter.
Business in the city was still brisk,
Only the Pound was quiet overnight.

Yet the mutterings had begun.
In park squares,
On wooden benches,
They were all talking to themselves.
It was very embarrassing,
Especially the noise of their love-making.

For, by now our love was neat,
Silent, economical, discreet.
Bans were enforced with justifiable violence,
Which made sound political sense.

Me and I were married in the end,
My best man, my Self, my only friend.
Together Triumphant Trinity,
How we ran this Great and Glorious Country
Down.

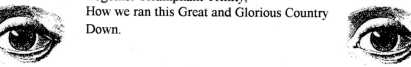

SOMETIMES IT'S ALL SO AMAZING

Sometimes it's all so amazing,
I want to fall at the feet of every singing pigeon,
Shopkeepers' conversation seems positively Shakespearean
And the sweet wrappers that flower down the street
Are perfectly arranged.

Sometimes it's all so amazing,
I could watch a tree like a TV,
Every leaf a brilliant documentary,
Each shadow as riveting as Inspector Morse.

Sometimes it's all so amazing,
I'll say kind things to people I can't even stand,
Look for the good in their face, heart and hand,
And find it.

Sometimes it's all so amazing,
Every day becomes a holy-day.
I could even pray
To bacon and eggs,
And a cup of tea is a spiritual experience!

Sometimes it's all so amazing,
I could say hello to a complete stranger,
Look into his eyes, let go my forever fear of danger
And just for a second, he would become my deepest friend.

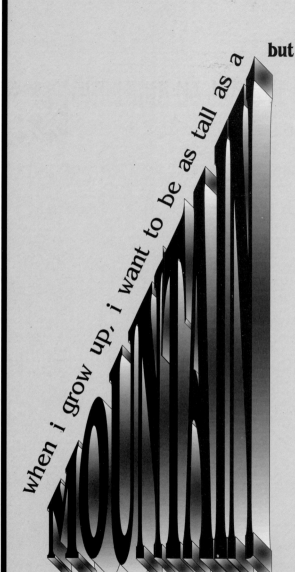

when i grow up, i want to be as tall as a **MOUNTAIN**

but what if I should fall

 O

 F

 F

 ?

A THROW AWAY POEM

I'm the Rubbish-Man,
Prince of Plastic, King of Tin Can.
People say I'm disgusting,
But the children are so trusting
When I rip {*or do they throw?*}
Such sweet wrappers out of their hands
To scatter them brightly across the lands.

I am the Reveller of Rags,
Emperor of Empty Shopping Bags.

Yes! I'm the Rubbish Man!
Catch me, Collar me, Collect me if you can.
It's me who stole into your sleep,
Took your mattress soft and deep.
Now, I'm coiled up, comfortably rusting by the Rubbish Stream
As She slips her way through the city's dark dream.

Oh! I'm the Rubbish Man!
Rubbing out wishes as only I can.
I made the blocks that burn the sky
And if you dare to ask me why,
I'll say it's my job, it's what I do.
Then will I dance The Rubbish Dance for you.

For, I'm the Rubbish Man!
Bin me, Bag me, Beat me if you can,
But together we'll dance all days away
And Darkness, my friend, shall come to stay.

HAD

GONE

work hard

He could go far, if only he would work hard.

I had been reported.
Next term, I tried to work hard,
Hard as a black road
Cut between the cars and the grass,
Hard as the nail that stole suddenly into wood,
Hard as Superman, the man of steel
Who lived on paper;
As hard as the best of the best,
The beans of the beans;
Harder than A and B
Hard as a C or even D
And sometimes the hardest, an E.

My alphabet was never good enough.
I worked hard as a house of cards,
But then it toppled,
Tumbling tears and I cried...

Cry Baby! Cry Baby! Na-na-na-na-na!
Softy! Softy! Softy-Softy-Softy!
What a woman! What a woman!

Being soft as a woman didn't work either.
So, instead of working hard,
I became hard;
Hard as boots, skinny trousers, skinny hair;
Hard as a stare.
And I ran from A, B, C, D and E
To live my life beginning with F,
If you know what I mean.

At last, I was the man of steel,
With a stolen boy inside.
That was hard, and lonely.
My skin was so tough though,
At last, like a snake I slipped out,
To grow into this man
With a woman in his heart.

LEAVING

I AM IN LOVE WITH ANN ELBOW

I met a Foot the other day.
We shook Toes.
I met a Nose not so long ago
And blew her a sloppy kiss.
Ever seen a Nose blush?
A Nostril flush?

Last night,
I met a pair of Eyes,
Hanging out behind the lids.
Shifty twins,
And right by their side
A nosy pair of Ears!
I really had to Leggit!

I met a Mouth this morning.
By Gum, he gave me lip!
And that cheeky Bum was so rude!
The Ankle Sisters such a strain
And when I met the Head,
She was a pain in the neck!

Just now,
I asked Anne Atter-Active Leg for a date,
But she stood me up
And now I'm so confused!

LAST NIGHT I SAW THE CITY BREATHING

AST night, I saw the City breathing:
Great Gusts of people,
Rushing in and
Puffing out
Of Stations' singing mouths

Last night, I saw the City laughing.
Take-Aways got the giggles,
Cinemas split their sides,
And Living Rooms completely creased themselves!

Last night, I saw the City dance.
Shadows were cheek to cheek with brick walls,
Trains wiggled their hips all over the place,
And the trees
In the breeze,
Put on a show for an audience of windows!

Last night, I saw the city starving,
Snaking Avenue smacked her lips
And swallowed seven roundabouts!
Fat office blocks got stuffed with light
And gloated over empty parking lots.

41

L **AST** night, I saw the City crying.
Cracked windows poured falling stars
And the streets were paved with mirrors.

Last night, I saw the City sit down at last.
Armchairs cuddled up to warm human beings
And a million cups of tea
Made best freinds with a million pairs of hands.

Last night, I saw the City sleeping
Roads night-dreamed,
Street Lamps quietly boasted,
'When I grow up, I'm going to be a star!'
And the Wind,
Like a cat,
Snoozed in the nooks of roofs.

AN

FOR MARC
{with love}

For when my brother dies
I shall cry tears of stone
Never will I have felt so alone
And my heart will try to be hard

For when my brother dies,
No more late night Monopoly and after
Bacon and eggs with a cup of laughter
The yolk of dawn just breaking

For when my brother dies
I shall cry a city of tears
Then put on a smile, hide all my fears
If only I could, if only

For when my brother dies
No more hate and family spite
Now I'm fine, everything's all right
But I will miss the making up

For when my brother dies
I shall cry blades of grass
People will be polite, dare not ask
Why my garden overgrows

For when my brother dies
I shall have no brother
No other to hug and to hold
And I the younger,
shall be the one who will grow old

43

POEMUM

NO MUM!

DON'T!

NO, NO NOT THE CHECKOUT ASSISTANT

PLeeeeeeeeeeeeeeeeeeeeeeeeeeeASE!

I GO TINNED TOMATO RED

WHEN SHE TALKS TO ANYONE

We're walking down the street and
AAAAAAAAAAAAAAAAAAAARGH!!!!
SHE'S SAYING SOMETHING FUNNY TO

A WOMAN WITH A DOG

IT'S REALLY LOUD

I HOPE NOBODY TURNS ROUND......

I GO GREEN AS A LETTUCE

MARK!

I WISH I WAS AS SMALL AS A LETTUCE

EVERYDAY SAYINGS

I married a door, how he screeched and whinged
Just couldn't handle it, became unhinged.

Married a chair, unlike any fable
He kept ending up under the table.

Married a mirror, you know, just to see!
He wasn't all he was cracked up to be.

So I fell in love with a tall, dark Cliff!
It was a long

           f
             a
               l l
                  ....if

Only I had stuck with Paperback Man,
Spineless! All words, ended like it began.

So, I hung out with a cute Coat-Hanger;
He was hung up, no more shall I hanker.

At last! I met the Curtain of my dreams.
It seems I was attracted to his seams.

Love drew us together, A love cloth-soft
Love could not be contained nor curtained off.
Love folded as night with rings for binding
Enfold us tonight, morning for finding
You...

THIS

BALLAD OF THE TREES

In your words, I am an Oak tree,
And I have been here a hundred years
Or more.
They tried to put me away in an old people's
home,
But I'm still hanging about in the street like a
tramp,
The earth is a good bed and
My blanket the wide sky.

Once,
I was round, small as your thumb
Until my mother dropped me,
Just like that.
I fell to the ground,
A dream inside a seed,
Waiting.

Then,
This street was stripped of its bark
And underneath lay the muddy drover's path.
Horses ploughed your classroom and
Barley grew between your desks.
It is so easy to forget.

Now,
In your words,
I am grown old.
The concrete hides me away,
And the street tries to run me over.
I wrap myself in bark
Against this biting wind.

But if you stop
And listen,
I shall promise to sing you a song of leaves
And if you dream,
Dream the cold hearted cities away, away
Dream the cold hearted cities away.